lingering thoughts

by christina lawson
a christina darling project

lingering thoughts

Printed in the United States.
Kindle Direct Publishing

ISBN: 9781688778832

Cover art designed by Matt Plumer
Layout and stills by Rachel Reneé

———————————

for more visit christinadarling.co

introduction

Everyone has a story to tell. This is a collection
of thoughts from a hopeless romantic battling
an eight-year addiction to love. A poetic guide
that leads you inside her emotional state of
mind. A mind filled with memories of romance,
hardships, and efforts to overcome her war with
heartache. This one is for those who have loved
so deeply, that the memory of a broken heart
still lingers on.

lingering thoughts

by christina lawson
a christina darling project

Dedicated to the one who had my heart.

Turning the page is always easiest,
but it is filling the spaces that give it meaning.

II

changes

The radio played.

Lyrics of Charles Bradley serenade
the confines of his car.

'I'm going through changes.'
These words so inherently loud,
they strum and tug at the heart.
She too has lost the best friend she had ever had.

Windows down,
too late now.

Breeze running through her fingers,
she reaches out.

She stays in this moment—
probably the last moments she'll have with him,
all the years shared in love together.

Driving past the city,
so quiet at night,
she feels the change in the air.

She glances over at him one last time,
closing her eyes,
daydreaming,
wishing this wasn't their last goodbye.

far from lucid

She lays on the bottom of her bedroom floor,
her eyes only moving to the flow of the ceiling fan above.

In a psychotic state, she stays;
she was drugged by his love,
her own dose of heroin,
an addiction she sadistically craved.

Paranoia creeps in,
slowly touching every part of her veins;
it spreads like wildfire.

Delusional.

Her thoughts now exploding off every possible scenario—
of what he might be doing now that he's gone,
every other female he might be fucking,
every other stolen kiss,
every conversation that was theirs to have,
now missed.

Down the rabbit hole she goes,
far from lucid,
her mind taken over by her broken heart again.

haunt me in my dreams

When one sleeps,
a gathering of dreams manifest.

Behind these resting eyes,
I am brought back to life,
dreaming of the impossible.
In an imaginary state of loving him, I go.

He comes to me like clockwork;
tall, broad and bearded.
His rugged hands reach out to me,
drawing me close.

As we float around the darkness that surrounds us,
my unconsciousness still pretends.
We stay in this moment,
caressing each other,
never wanting it to end.

Before he goes,
our eyes both lock-in.
Leaning in silently,
he whispers to me,
'Don't worry. I will always be here.'

Refusing to let go;
I try and hold on to this moment,
even when I know,
I know
he will soon be out of daytime's reach,
for when I wake,
it was only a dream—
knowing he was just a dream,
my dream.

spinning

Roundabout we go,
spinning wheels built on jagged edges full of sorrow.

As the day goes by,
the wheels slowly steady—
steady for one's reach.

But be careful now or feel his bite,
a restless mind will take its flight.

Foolish and impatient.
How much more can one take?
All one wants is for consciousness to break
this stagnant turn of uncertainty.

VII

conversations in bed

Conversations in bed.
Half-naked, we lay.

You glance over to me
and with those three words, you say,
'I love you.'

You begin to touch me,
our bodies now one.
You kiss me.
It was this night when I felt our souls connect.
I completely came undone.

Your words kept me fed,
nourishing me inevitably.
You led me to believe we once would be wed.

On and off, we always were.
Weakness took hold in between the sheets,
staring back at me with those hazel eyes
and imprinting my soul.
My heart still weeps.

In between the sheets,
our fantasy would stay
until that day—
when you could no longer continue,
with our romantic foreplay.

IX

10.10.10

On the eve of our October night,
I think of you—
an eight-year dream,
living in the in-between.

Some days so good,
we knew we could,
but those days grew sour,
never easily devoured.

Like you forever,
love you always.
Once my world,
now just words.

On the eve of our night,
I'm stuck here just thinking of you.

strangers

Lovers,
now strangers,
darkened with sadness—
But this is how we chose it to be,
knowing that day would come,
realizing we are better off...
free.

self-torture through song

Our song came on the radio—
second time this week.
Probably should change it.
I try and tune out the lyrics,
but Ray LaMontagne's voice makes me weak.

Our song—
the one we listened to the first time sitting on my mother's
couch,
a flashback to a time where our love was new—
now thinking about it,
makes it hard to chew.

Ah, the chorus sings,
'you are the best thing.'

But really—
were you the best thing that ever happened to me?

Three minutes and fifty-two seconds of torture
bleed through my eardrums.
Already numb,
I continue to let it play.

I adjust the volume.
Finally,
the last lines of the chorus.
Self-torture.
But hey,
it's the price I'm willing to pay,
traveling down memory lane.

that place

Take me to that place,
where you and I are meant to be.
I never asked for you to set me free.

Take me to that place,
just you and me forever,
where we can grow old together.

A place where we can see our love
hovering from above.
Like the stars in the sky,
we shine.

Take me to that place where you were mine.

Take me to that place where our love never dies,
where there are no goodbyes.

our masterpiece

Let me paint a picture of a time,
where the memory of us stood still,
just you and I,
alone.

Dancing in the night's darkness,
alongside an abandoned city street.

The stroke of the brush captures,
the broken traffic lights flickering in our direction.

Shadows of a spotlight form.
We take center stage.

The sounds of the city would play behind us.
We, the conductors of our very own symphonic orchestra.

While the drops of every color are so intricately placed,
pigments of time will portray,
when we, the two lovers,
slowly became our very own canvas.

A canvas of a beautiful masterpiece
of a moment
that will forever be encased.

fleeting

Her love so bright,
she gave me sight.

Be still my darling.
Don't leave.
I will hold you tight.

Away she goes with no goodbye.
Away she goes into the night,
for she was once mine,
my sweet appetite.

broken

She sits there with her

abandoned heart—

bruised,

b r o k e n ,

torn apart.

All she wanted was

for him to be proud,

to love her quietly,
to love her loud.

Time has passed,
days are long.

Deserted, she stays.

She's left there wondering
what all went wrong.

XIX

loving you should be lethal

Loving you should be lethal.
Someone come tie me up and throw away the key.
A love-struck criminal on the run.
A mastermind of her own misery
always coming undone.
Homicidal hopeless romantic
gone manic.

It's okay.
No one panic.

the disappearing act

Outside I sit.
Another season is about to hit,
the rain quietly falling,
a sound so peaceful it keeps me calm—
the only calm I have felt in days.

I'm fighting off the frustrations of losing you,
mind-fucked in so many ways.

Back and forth I sway on our old rocking chairs,
the ones that sat in the home we shared—
But do you even remember or fucking care?

I sink below in my chair.
Closing my eyes, I try to think of you
but as the hours pass,
I didn't realize how late the night grew.

The memory of you starts to fade,
a disappearing act by you, my darling,
that you were always so incredibly great at.

heartbreak

He stands there feeding away at my sorrows,
the master manipulator.

He disguised himself as hope;
the accomplice of heartbreak.

As he feeds,
he starts to tear away at my soul.
He bites down deep,
biting on bits and pieces of nostalgia.

Aren't there other parts he'd rather indulge in?

That inconsiderate fool.
Why can't he just let me keep those savory moments?
Let me continue to romanticize about the past,
to fantasize about all the good times that I thought would last.

Shh… don't remind me about the bad,
the arguments.
No more love… So what?
I know what we had.

This is what he does.
He enjoys preying on the weak.
Help me find strength;
I must stay strong and on my feet.

Can I die from a broken heart?

Hoping one day I'll survive this mend,
he continues to drain me dry.
How much more can this last?
I continue to cry.

Devouring a little more,
he wipes his mouth clean.

For I know he will come back tomorrow
to finish his nightly routine.

romantically self-destructive

There is beauty in this broken chaos that consumes me,
where anticipation guides the mind into complete anxiety—

holding steady,
breathing heavy,
finding its way back down below into the heart.

Sharp pain,
tight grip,
eyes closed,
lie there - don't move.
This too will soon pass,
I suppose.

Breathing in,
breathing out,
the pain subsides,
fighting the mind's obscurities.
Wasting away amongst the fray,
lonely I will stay.

breathe

Breathe
as the walls cave in;
catching
every
last
breath.

her reality

Broken glass lay shattered on the floor,
glass from a picture frame that once held

A reflection of our time together,
a reflection of two shadows:
one a dream,
the other her reality.

A time where her expectations were never his reality,
time in which a river flows from her past,
lying there in pieces inside that broken glass.

her unmated departure

If she dies before she marries,
please bury her in the whitest gown.

Upon this dark beauty,
will sit the coldest of crowns.

Place thee in a four-square casket,
surrounded in mahogany.

Death will read her as the
hopeless romantic who feared monogamy,
admired for her charm,
destroyed by love's harm.

When that time comes,
nature will kiss her six feet under,
buried beneath the earth,
singing the sweetest of life's wonders.

error

User denied.
He loved her by default.

Loving himself more than she,
he forgot to read the user's manual,
on how to be with a woman,
to love her even through her malfunctions.

Artificial intelligence.

Not understanding each piece that makes her
fully functional.

Visually aesthetic,
but complex within her system—
each bit of machinery,
wire,
carefully creating an ecosystem that could combust,
given the right opportunity.

He carefully tries to fix the pieces that would break again,
but mistakenly forgets how to nurture or maintain.

Error.
He begins again.

curious

Drawn to the darkness,
her heart grew wild.
No fear could tame her.

XXXIII

unafraid

This emotion holds steady
like a man walking a tightrope,
balanced,
heavy,

clear to the sight of eyes.
It washes over me.
Holding on, I grip my hands,
I brace for impact:

f-i-v-e,
f-o-u-r,
t-h-r-e-e,
t-w-o.

ONE.

I let go.
I surrender myself,
unafraid.
I begin again.

the dissection

It's when the night's air is quiet and still,
I can hear the jaded rhythms of my heartbeat play for me.

I pull back the layers,
the deep tissue scars that got me here.

Slowly—
I dissect every part of this bruised vessel.

Reaching in deep,
I try and clasp the remaining pieces
that hurt the most.

Careful now,
I don't want to remove what has healed:
the parts that give me hope,
the parts that keep this red vessel afloat.

As I dispose of the final remains,
the tarnished and unfamiliar pieces
that no longer hold purpose,
the heart begins to play again
playing a cathartic melody.

It starts over,
and I begin.

i bid you adieu

It was on that very mountain,
amongst the beauty of the stars,
where she bid him adieu,
for he was no longer
the journey she wanted to climb.

closure...

It's been a long time coming.
Closure can mean a lot of things for different people.

Closure comes in strides.

One day,
feeling on top of the world.
The next,
crying on the bathroom floor,
wondering if you'll ever love again.

Closure...
The ending of a chapter,
the beginning of something new,
the feeling of a resurgence
like a phoenix rising from the ashes.

Closure...
The retracing of what once was,
now numb for days.

Closure...
Self-help books?

Closure...
Hating but still glimpsing backward
to the love you once gave.

Closure...
Replacing them with someone else.

Closure...
Moving on isn't easy,
and maybe closure won't come in a day,
so with the moments shared with oneself,
honor the past
and transition for the limitations
you can and will sustain one day.

Closure.

Made in the USA
Middletown, DE
29 September 2020

20398124R00031